C000182820

● soho
● theatre company

Soho Theatre Company presents

WRONG PLACE

by **Mark Norfolk**

First performed at Soho Theatre on 2 October 2003

Performances in the Lorenz Auditorium

Soho Theatre is supported by

 **Bloomberg**

Registered Charity No: 267234

Soho Theatre Company has the support of the Pearson Playwrights' Scheme sponsored by The Peggy Ramsay Foundation.

WRONG PLACE
by **Mark Norfolk**

Monty	Geoffrey Burton
Trevor	Mark Theodore
Roddy	Larrington Walker
Director	Abigail Morris
Assistant Director	Joe Austin
Designer	Naomi Wilkinson
Lighting Designer	Jason Taylor
Sound Designer	John Leonard
Production Manager	Nick Ferguson
Stage Manager	Andrea Grey
Deputy Stage Manager	Helen King
Assistant Stage Manager	Sally Higson
Chief Technician	Nick Blount
Chief Electrician	Christoph Wagner
Lighting Technician	Ade Peterkin
Scenery built and painted by	Robert Knight
Casting	Ginny Schiller

Soho Theatre would like to thank:
Model train set kindly donated by Hornby
Davidoff Lights supplied by Propaganda
Thameslink Rail Ltd

Advertising: MandH Advertising
Graphic Design: Jane Harper
Photography: Barry Rosenthal / Susa Scalora / Getty Images
Photo montage: Jane Harper

Soho Theatre and Writers' Centre
21 Dean Street
London W1D 3NE
Admin: 020 7287 5060
Fax: 020 7287 5061
Box Office: 020 7478 0100
www.sohotheatre.com
email: box@sohotheatre.com

THE COMPANY

Cast

Geoffrey Burton Monty

Theatre credits include *Driving Miss Daisy* (English Theatre Frankfurt and Theatre Royal, Bury St. Edmunds – national tour); *Huis Clos, One for the Road* (Old Bull Arts Centre); *Ravaged Shakespeare* (St George's Theatre); *A Taste of Honey, This Property is Condemned, Red Eye of Love, The Negro Giant, For Esme with Love of Squalor, The Death of Bessie Smith* (Off Broadway); *Spring in Manhattan, Pyjama Game* (All-Souls Players, NY City); *Death Watch, Catcher in the Rye, Zoo Story* and *Spoon River Anthology* (Gene Frankel Rep. Theatre).

Mark Theodore Trevor

Theatre credits include *Dirty Butterfly* (Soho Theatre); *Rumblefish* (World Stage Premiere and national tour for Pilot Theatre Co); *A Bitter Herb* (Theatre Royal, Bristol Old Vic); *Edmond and the Collection* (Northern Stage Ensemble) and *Measure for Measure* (RNT). Television credits include *Casualty* (BBC); *The Bill* (Pearson) and *Queer as Folk* (Red Productions). Film credits include *Ali G in da House* (Working Title) and *NOD* (Bart Productions).

Larrington Walker Roddy

Theatre credits include *Whistle down the Wind* (No 1 Tour); *The Free State* (Birmingham Rep. and tour); *The Merchant of Venice* (West Yorkshire Playhouse); *Lost in the Stars* (New Sussex Opera – Brighton); *Week In Week Out* (Foco Novo / Soho Poly); *Old Time Story* (Theatre Royal, Stratford East); *The Beggars Opera, Guys and Dolls* (National Theatre); *One Fine Day, Black Man's Burden* (Riverside Studios); *One Rule, Jesus Christ Superstar* (Palace Theatre); *The Wizard of Oz* and *White Suit Blues* (Nottingham Playhouse). Television credits include *The Bill* (BBC); *Thin Air, You and Me, Drums along Balmoral Drive, Fighting Back, Dead Ahead, Moon over Soho* and *Waterloo Sunset* (BBC). Film credits include *Human Traffic, Burning Illusion* and *Lamb*.

Company

Joe Austin Assistant Director

Joe trained in Music and Drama at Hull University. Past theatre direction includes *Protection* (Soho Theatre); *Phaedra's Love, Gosforth's Fete, Mother Figure* (Birmingham Theatre School); *Roberto Zucco* (National Student Drama Festival, Scarborough); *Skylight* (Donald Roy Theatre, Hull) and *Zoo Story* (Gulbenkian Studio, Hull). Musical direction includes *Much Ado About Nothing, Arabian Nights* (Donald Roy Theatre, Hull) and *The Visit* (Z Theatre, Edinburgh).

John Leonard Sound Designer

John started working in theatre sound over thirty years ago. He has worked in theatres all over the world for many organisations and producers, including the Royal Shakespeare Company, where he was Head of Sound and an Associate Artist. He received a Drama Desk award for his work on *Madea* (Broadway), is the author of numerous articles and an acclaimed book on theatre sound design and was named Theatre Sound Designer of The Year at the 2002 Entertainment Technology Show (Las Vegas). John is Sound Consultant for the Almeida Theatre and a Director of Aura Sound Design Ltd. Previous work for Soho Theatre Company includes *A Reckoning, Kiss Me Like You Mean It, Office, Meeting Myself Coming Back* and *Things You Shouldn't Say Past Midnight.*

Abigail Morris Director

Abigail Morris has been Artistic Director of Soho Theatre since 1992. Productions include *Protection, Things You Shouldn't Say Past Midnight, Office* (also at Edinburgh International Festival)*; Kiss Me Like You Mean It, Navy Pier, The Station, Be My Baby* (at Soho Theatre / national tour); *Waking, Tulip Futures, The Rock Station* and *Kindertransport* (at the Cockpit, West End and Manhattan Theatre Club, New York). Abigail was also the founder of Trouble and Strife Theatre Company, where her productions included the award winning plays *Present Continuous, Now and at the Hour of our Death, Next to you I Lie* (Co-writer and Director) and various operas including Britten's *Noye's Fluddle* (Royal Albert Hall and Festival Hall); *Julius Caesar Jones* (Sadlers Wells) and Cole Porter's *Leave it to Me* (Arts Theatre, Cambridge).

Mark Norfolk Writer

Mark Norfolk first studied Speech and Drama at Middlesex Polytechnic, appearing on stage, TV and screen before working as a journalist. He then went on to study Independent Film and in 2001 completed his debut feature film called *Love is not Enough.* Mark was a Writer in Attachment at the Soho Theatre & Writer's Centre in 2002 during which he wrote

Wrong Place. His play *Knock Down Ginger* opened the Premio Candoni Arte Terme in Italy in 2002, was a selection in the International Playwriting Festival in 2001 and was on the shortlist for the Verity Bargate Award in 2000. *Knock Down Ginger* received support from the Peggy Ramsay Foundation and was shown at the Warehouse Theatre in June 2003 directed by Jeffrey Kissoon. Another of Mark's plays *Fair as the Dark Get* made the shortlist for the Alfred Fagon Award in 1998.

Jason Taylor Lighting Designer

Recent and current work includes *Protection* (Soho Theatre); *Us and Them* (Hampstead Theatre); *Hobson's Choice, Yerma* (Royal Exchange Theatre); *Abigail's Party* (New Ambassadors, Whitehall); *Pretending to be me* (Comedy Theatre); *Little Shop of Horrors* (West Yorkshire Playhouse); *My Night with Reg / Dealer's Choice* (Birmingham Rep); *The Clearing* (Shared Experience); *Single Spies, Sitting Pretty, Pirates Of Penzance* (national tour); *Office* (Edinburgh International Festival); *Hedda Gabler, Snake in Fridge* (Royal Exchange Theatre); *The Dead Eye Boy* (Hampstead Theatre) and *Iolanthe, The Mikado* and *Yeoman of the Guard* (Savoy Theatre). Jason has lit over 150 other productions including *Fourteen Seasons at the Open Air Theatre, Kindertransport* (Vaudeville Theatre); *Rosencrantz and Guildenstren* (Piccadilly Theatre); *And Then There Were None* (Duke Of York's Theatre) and *Great Balls of Fire* (Cambridge Theatre). Jason was also Lighting Consultant for the new Soho Theatre, London and the Open Air Theatre, Regents Park.

Naomi Wilkinson Designer

Naomi trained at the Motely Theatre Design Course after a BA (Hons) in Fine Art at Bristol Polytechnic. Recent theatre credits include *I Weep at my Piano* (BAC); *Happy Birthday Mr Decka D* (Traverse Theatre); *Shoot me in the Heart* (Gate Theatre); *I Can't Wake Up* (Lyric Theatre Studio); *Aladdin* (Lyric Hammersmith); *A Little Fantasy* (Soho Theatre); *The Firework Makers' Daughter* (Sheffield Crucible) all for the Told by an Idiot, *Gobbledygook* (Gogmagogs, Traverse Theatre); *Don't Look Back* (Dreamthinkspeak, Brighton Festival); *Mules, My Life in the Bush of Ghosts* and *Heredity* (all Royal Court Theatre); *The Prince of Homberg* (NT Studio); *It's Only a Game Show* (First Person Dance Co); *Well Farewell* and *Witch Hunt* (Brouhaha, BAC); *Two Horsemen* (Gate Theatre and Bush Theatre) and *Snake House* (Greenwich Theatre Studio).

● soho
● theatre company

Soho is passionate in its commitment to new writing, producing a year-round programme of bold, original and accessible new plays – many of them from first-time playwrights.

'a foundry for new talent... one of the country's leading producers of new writing' Evening Standard

Soho aims to be the first port of call for the emerging writer and combines the process of production with the process of development. The unique Writers' Centre invites writers at any stage of their career to submit scripts and receives, reads and reports on over 2,000 per year. In addition to the national Verity Bargate Award – a competition aimed at new writers – it runs an extensive series of programmes from the innovative Under 11's Scheme, Young Writers' Group (14-25s) and Westminster Prize (encouraging local writers) to a comprehensive Workshop Programme and Writers' Attachment Scheme working to develop writers not just in the theatre but also for radio, TV and film.

'a creative hotbed... not only the making of theatre but the cradle for new screenplay and television scripts' The Times

Contemporary, comfortable, air-conditioned and accessible, the Soho Theatre is busy from early morning to late at night. Alongside the production of new plays, it's also an intimate venue to see leading comedians from the UK and US in an eclectic programme mixing emerging new talent with established names. Soho Theatre is home to Café Lazeez, serving delicious Indian fusion dishes downstairs with a lively bar upstairs that has a 1am licence.

'London's coolest theatre by a mile' Midweek

Soho Theatre Company is developing its work outside of the building and expanding the scope of its work with writers. It hosts the annual Soho Writers' Festival in November – now in its fourth year – which brings together innovative practitioners from the creative industries with writers working in theatre, film, TV, radio, literature and poetry. Our programme aims to challenge, entertain and inspire writers and audiences from all backgrounds.

● soho
● theatre company

Soho Theatre and Writers' Centre
21 Dean Street, London W1D 3NE
Admin: 020 7287 5060 Fax: 020 7287 5061
Box Office: 020 7478 0100 Minicom: 020 7478 0136
www.sohotheatre.com   email: box@sohotheatre.com

Bars and Restaurant
Café Lazeez brasserie serves Indian-fusion dishes until 12pm. Late bar open until 1am. The Terrace Bar serves a range of soft and alcoholic drinks.

Email information list
For regular programme updates and offers, join our free email information list by emailing box@sohotheatre.com
If you would like to make any comments about any of the productions seen at Soho Theatre, why not visit our chatroom at www.sohotheatre.com?

Hiring the theatre
Soho Theatre has a range of rooms and spaces for hire. Please contact the theatre managers on 020 7287 5060 or email hires@sohotheatre.com for further details.

● soho
● theatre company

Artistic Director: Abigail Morris
Assistant to Artistic Director: Nadine Hoare
Administrative Producer: Mark Godfrey
Assistant to Administrative Producer: Tim Whitehead
Writers' Centre Director: Nina Steiger
Associate Director: Jonathan Lloyd
Casting Director: Ginny Schiller
Marketing and Development Director: Zoe Reed
Development Officer: Gayle Rogers
Marketing Officer: Ruth Waters
Marketing and Development Assistant: Kelly Duffy
Press Officer: Nancy Poole (020 7478 0142)
General Manager: Catherine Thornborrow
Front of House and Building Manager: Anne Mosley
Financial Controller: Kevin Dunn
Box Office Manager: Kate Truefitt
Deputy Box Office Manager: Steve Lock
Box Office Assistants: Darren Batten, Richard Gay, Brett McCallum, Leah Read, William Sherriff Hammond, Natalie Worrall and Miranda Yates
Duty Managers: Morag Brownlie, Mike Owen and Kate Ryan
Front of House Staff: Rachel Bavidge, Helene Le Bohec, Sharon Degen, Claire Fowler, Matthew Halpin, Sioban Hyams, Grethe Jensen, Ian Marshall, Neil Maclennan, Lizzie McCallum, Claire Randall, Katherine Smith, Rebecca Storey, Luke Tebbutt, Kat Smith, and Jamie Zubairi
Production Manager: Nick Ferguson
Chief Technician: Nick Blount
Chief LX: Christoph Wagner
Lighting Technician: Ade Peterkin

THE SOHO THEATRE DEVELOPMENT CAMPAIGN

Soho Theatre Company receives core funding from Westminster City Council and Arts Council England, London. In order to provide as diverse a programme as possible and expand our audience development and outreach work, we rely upon additional support from trusts, foundations, individuals and business.

All our major sponsors share a common commitment to developing new areas of activity and encouraging creative partnerships between business and the arts.

If you would like to find out more about supporting Soho Theatre, please contact Gayle Rogers, Development Officer on 020 7478 0111 or email gayle@sohotheatre.com.

We are immensely grateful to all of our sponsors and donors for their support and commitment.

Sponsors: Bloomberg, Getty Images, TBWA\GGT **Major Supporters:** Calouste Gulbenkian Foundation • Esmeé Fairbairn Foundation • The Foyle Foundation • The Paul Hamlyn Foundation • John Lyon's Charity • Roger and Cecil Jospé • The Harold Hyam Wingate Foundation • Roger Wingate **Education Patrons:** Tony and Rita Gallagher • Nigel Gee **Trusts and Foundations:** Anon • Delfont Foundation • The Fishmongers' Company • The Follett Trust • The Hazel Wood Charitable Trust • The Samuel Goldwyn Foundation • JG Hogg Charitable Trust • Hyde Park Place Estate Charity • Linbury Trust • Mathilda and Terence Kennedy Charitable Trust • The St James's Trust • The Kobler Trust • The Really Useful Theatres • Tesco Charity Trust • Unity Theatre Trust **Patrons:** Anon • Richard Borchard • Katie Bradford • Julie & Robert Breckman • Rob Brooks • David Day • Raphael Djanogly • John Drummond • Samuel French Ltd • Madeleine Hamel • Jack and Linda Keenan • Solid Management • Richard Willson OBE • Paul and Pat Zatz **Studio Seats:** Anon • Jo Apted • Peter Backhouse • Leslie Bolsom • Mrs Alan Campbell-Johnson • David Day • Raphael Djanogly • Imtiaz and Susan Dossa • Anthony Gardner • Catherine Graham-Harrison and Nicholas Warren • Sally A Graudons • Hope Hardcastle • Roger Jospé • Jeremy Levison • John and Jean McCaig • Annie Parker • Eric and Michèle Senat • Simonetta Valentini • Marc Vlessing

SOHO THEATRE and WRITERS' CENTRE
In 1996, Soho Theatre Company was awarded an £8 million Lottery grant from the Arts Council of England to help create the Soho Theatre + Writers' Centre. An additional £2.6 million in matching funds was raised and over 500 donors supported the capital appeal. The full list of supporters is displayed on our website at www.sohotheatre.com/thanks.htm and on the thank you door at the entrance to the theatre.

BUILDING SUPPORTERS
Supported by the Arts Council of England with National Lottery funds
The Lorenz Auditorium supported by Carol and Alan Lorenz
Rooms: The Education and Development Studio supported by the Foundation for Sport and the Arts • Equity Trust Fund Green Room • The Vicky Arenson Writers' Seminar Room • Writers' Room supported by The Samuel Goldwyn Foundation • Unity Theatre Writers' Room • Writers' Room supported by Nick Hornby and Annette Lynton Mason • The Marchpole Dressing Room • Wardrobe supported by Angels the Costumiers • The Peter Sontar Production Office • The White Light Control Room • The Strand Dimmer Room • The Dennis Selinger Meeting Room
Building: The Esmée Fairbairn Foundation • The Rose Foundation • The Meckler Foundation • Roberta Sacks
Soho first: BAFTA • Cowboy Films Ltd • Simons Muirhead & Burton
Gold patrons: Eric Abraham • Jill and Michael Barrington • Roger Bramble • Anthony and Elizabeth Bunker • John Caird • David and Pat Chipping • John Cohen at Clintons • Nadia and Mark Crandall • David Day • Michael and Maureen Edwards • Charles Hart • Hat Trick Productions • David Huyton at Moore Stephens • Miriam and Norman Hyams • David Jackson at Pilcher Hershman • The St James' Trust • John Kelly–European Quality • Mr and Mrs Philip Kingsley • The McKenna Charitable Trust • Nancy Meckler and David Aukin • Michael and Mimi Naughton • Robert Ogden CBE • Diana Quick • Christian Roberts • Lyn Schlesinger • Peter M Schlesinger • Carl Teper • Diana and Richard Toeman • Richard Wilson OBE • Margaret Wolfson

Registered Charity: 267234

First published in 2003 by Oberon Books Ltd.
(incorporating Absolute Classics)
521 Caledonian Road, London N7 9RH
Tel: 020 7607 3637 / Fax: 020 7607 3629

e-mail: oberon.books@btinternet.com
www.oberonbooks.com

A catalogue record for this book is available from the British
Library.

ISBN: 1 84002 400 3

Cover photo: Barry Rosenthal / Susa Scalora / Getty Images

Photo montage: Jane Harper

Printed in Great Britain by Antony Rowe Ltd, Chippenham.

Characters

MONTY GRIFFITHS
TREVOR CHARLES
RODDY CHARLES

The author would like to thank
Jonathan Lloyd, Jason Rose and Rolando McNish
for all their help during the writing of this play

Scene 1

Lights up on the Visitors Room of a prison, cold, clinical.

Two men are in the room, MONTY GRIFFITHS, a smartly dressed black man, early to mid sixties, and TREVOR CHARLES, a black man aged mid to late twenties. TREVOR is agitated.

TREVOR: What now? What am I gonna do? What am I gonna do? C'mon, what do I do?

He calms down a little.

I don't know what to do, man. I don't know what to do. I mean, whaddya think?

MONTY: You just got to…use your head, man.

TREVOR: So what is it? What… I mean, what's the…

MONTY: Hold it down.

TREVOR: Nah, man, This aint… I mean, I aint done nothin', you get me. I've done nothin', man. This aint right, this just aint right.

MONTY: You think I don't know that? I know it's not right.

TREVOR: So what, I mean…

MONTY: You just got to…

TREVOR: Na na na na na…

MONTY: Just have to settle.

TREVOR: It aint fuckin' right.

MONTY: Settle.

TREVOR: How the fuck…

There's a long pause.

MONTY: Your solicitor…

TREVOR: It's Cummins, Rupert Cummins. He's alright, he knows the runnings. One time I got grab up for driving – no paperwork. Cummins come down and he convinced them that I was an apprentice mechanic taking this 2.5 litre, 320 brake horse power Sierra Cosworth for a test drive. I was doing sixty in a thirty mile zone. Nice set of wheels that was.

MONTY: You get through?

TREVOR: Walked it mate. Not even a caution. Only thing though, Cummins was so good, a couple of them detectives booked their cars in for a service, you get me.

MONTY: (*Pause.*) So what happen, what did he say, this Cummins?

TREVOR: Usual stuff…gonna do this gonna do that.

MONTY: Let me get someone for you.

TREVOR: Nah, man, save your money. I just wanna get out of here.

MONTY: You got to be careful…don't do anything stupid.

TREVOR: Like what?

MONTY: You know how some of them man go on like them is a public defender when all the time…

TREVOR: What d'you take me for?

MONTY: Just got to use your head.

TREVOR: I'm doing that. That's what I'm doing. Using my head, keeping cool, trying to keep cool. But it aint easy, you get me. It aint easy in here.

MONTY: It's not easy.

TREVOR: With my form? Them mans say they're gonna throw the book at me. I can't do it, man. I don't think I can…this place…no more.

MONTY: Trevor…

TREVOR: My kids, man. (*Pause.*) Went to the zoo that day, you know that? Yeah, cost me a fortune. But my boy wanted to see the lions. He's been wantin' to go since his birthday three months ago. Didn't make it then 'cos his mum was just… Jenny, man, she was just givin' it to me, givin' me grief…money, this, that an' the other. Women, man. (*Beat.*) Anyway, the youth was well hyped up, jumpin' around, 'I'm goin' zoo, I'm goin' zoo.' But that day it was rainin', pourin' with rain. Rain rain rain rain rain. Stood there for ages, just waitin', getting soaked. But them lions weren't comin' out that day. The boy start to bawl. Real tears, man. Them kinda' tears that get you, you know…get you right here. If I coulda' got in that cage, I woulda' dragged them lions out, 'bout you're king of the jungle. Look how you frighten of a little bit of English rain.' Little man cryin', I had to pull him up. I told him, I said, 'Sometimes Romie, we don't always get what we want.' I promised to take him again when it aint rainin'. How am I gonna do that now?

MONTY reads one of the safety signs on the wall.

MONTY: I hate these places. I hate the smell.

MONTY fishes a pack of cigarettes from his jacket pocket.

TREVOR: You can't do that, you know.

MONTY: Eh?

TREVOR points to a NO SMOKING sign on the wall.

TREVOR: No smoking.

MONTY: It's alright, man. Want one? Go on, take one, man.

TREVOR accepts a cigarette. MONTY lights it for him.

They used to lock people up for anythin' when I first come to this country. Prisons were full, full of white man. (*Beat.*) Them white man start to sing when the black man arrive. You see, they saw that the black man is hardworkin', like to work hard. An' them believe that soon he will work his way up to the top. An' no way could they find themselves below him. So them start to throw them in jail. Throw them in jail so…bam bam bam!

They smoke in silence for a moment.

C'mere, man.

They hug.

You alright though?

TREVOR: Yeah.

MONTY: Cool?

TREVOR: That's me. That's what I'm doin'. But it aint easy.

MONTY: Everythin' will be alright.

TREVOR: Don't be tellin' me that, man. It's alright for you, you're on street.

MONTY: What I'm tryin' to tell you is that them use jail to control we. An' sometimes a man can get confused. You know that every black family in this country know somebody in jail?

TREVOR: Eh?

MONTY: How do we defeat them?

TREVOR: I dunno.

MONTY: C'mon man?

TREVOR: Keep cool.

MONTY: Good boy. Good boy.

Fade down lights.

Scene 2

The Prison Visitors Room.

TREVOR sits, waiting patiently. Enter RODDY CHARLES hurriedly. He's a black man, early sixties, dressed in a Railtrack staff uniform. They shake hands.

RODDY: The eight twenty-five Haywards Heath jump the lane at East Croydon. Bloody kids think it's a joke to throw things on the line. (*Beat.*) You alright?

TREVOR: Yeah.

RODDY: It's a good thing that train slow down comin' through the station. Look, I never even get a chance to go home an' take off my uniform.

TREVOR: Didn't get nothin' on the news.

RODDY: Yeah, man, the Gatwick line block both ways. Passengers mad as hell cos them can't get to the airport. I had was to call out Transport Police. Them lazy buggers, all them do all day is sit in office drinkin' tea.

TREVOR: They catch anyone?

RODDY: Them? No, man. One ugly white man ask me when the next train. Man ugly, you see. Favour that man…what's that film, the one with all the little pickpocket boys?

TREVOR: What film?

RODDY: That actor, what's his name now?

TREVOR: Pickpocket boys?

RODDY: My memory not so good anymore. I can't remember things. The man have a big nose an' him teeth black.

TREVOR: Don't know.

RODDY: Ever get that when all day you can't remember something? But as I lay my head down at night – it hit me.

TREVOR: The brain stores it in the back there.

RODDY: This thing's botherin' me now. The man's a drunkard, like, live with a woman, Nancy…

TREVOR: Nancy? I know, I know…

RODDY: An' them have a little short leg dog.

TREVOR: I got it, Oliver Twist.

RODDY: Aaah, that's it, Oliver Twist. I'm gettin' old y'see.

TREVOR: Na, it's still there, but the brain's thinkin' about other things more important, y'get me.

RODDY: You think so?

TREVOR: Yeah, yeah, I read that somewhere.

RODDY: That man with the big nose…

TREVOR: Fagin.

RODDY: Ah, Fagin, that's him. You know that's the first movie I take her to see uptown. That was '69. Dress up in my new suit. I did want to make an impression. But little bit I start to bawl in the picture house. Yessir, I love that movie. Oliver Twist. Alec Guinness, that's his name don't it?

TREVOR: Yeah. He's dead.

RODDY: He was a very good actor. Play that part, the Jews them never like it, but he act that part good. Yeah man, Fagin, that's what that ugly man look like. Same way. Big nose, black teeth, hair push to one side.

TREVOR: Was he one of them Jewish, orthodox…?

RODDY: Don't know about that. The man just plain ugly. Him ask me what time the next Brighton. I say I don't know, an' as him walk away him call me nigger.

TREVOR: Yeah?

RODDY: An' the man so ugly.

TREVOR: What did you do?

RODDY: What me to do?

TREVOR: Box him down, man.

RODDY: I tell him to fuck off. An' the man demand to see the station manager.

TREVOR: What, Reddington?

RODDY: Reddington tell me off right in front of this ugly man. I vex!

TREVOR: All a man like him, I woulda' drop for sure, you get me.

RODDY: An' you know that ugly man deny him call me a nigger.

TREVOR: Na man, don't tell me them things.

RODDY: I tell him, You not only ugly but you is a damn liard. An' Reddington come put his hands 'pon me. I said, 'Take your fuckin' hands off me.' Him say, 'That's a warning.' I say, 'Piss off.' Him say, 'That's a second warning, that's a second warning…'

TREVOR: Na man…

RODDY: Transport Police come. That man, Steve, from Scotland – nobody know what the hell him talkin' about, his accent so thick – 'A'raight Roddy? Caam-doun, come-wi-me.' He take me into his office an' gimme a cuppa tea.

TREVOR: Reddington, man.

RODDY: (*Beat.*) The truth is, I have less than a year to go. Lose my pension, thirty odd years count for nothin'. You know how many black men I see lose them lives shuntin' trains? Now I find myself walkin' around on the platform in a nice clean suit. But they don't want old dinosaurs, much less old black dinosaurs like me. (*Beat.*) It's all market forces, shareholders, accumulative profit. They want speculators, money-men, that's all they care about. (*Indignantly.*) I built that fuckin' railway. My blood an' sweat lies on that track. They can't take that away from me. (*Pause.*) Steve Reddington knows nothin' about trains. Come there with a university degree an' think he's better than everybody.

TREVOR: I know where the cunt lives.

RODDY: You in enough trouble as it is. (*Pause.*) Bwoy, I could do with the toilet, you know.

TREVOR: It's through there.

RODDY: As you get old you're always desperate to go but when you get in there, nothin' come out. Can't squeeze a drop. One man at the station, little Bajan fellow named Simpson, he calls it the prostrate.

They laugh.

The Prostrate, you know.

TREVOR: I heard nuff man is droppin' dead from that shit.

RODDY: Simpson say, 'The prostrate is a form of revenge, where your balls turn in on you an' nyam out the whole of your crutch.'

TREVOR laughs.

TREVOR: Prostrate.

RODDY: He's a funny man, that Simpson.

TREVOR: It's through there. Turn right at the end of the corridor.

RODDY: Let me wait.

Pause.

TREVOR: Mum, she…?

RODDY: She in the car.

TREVOR: You leave her in the car?

RODDY: I leave her in the car? She don't wanna come in.

TREVOR: There's a cafe here.

RODDY: She don't wanna set foot in the building.

Pause.

TREVOR: So what – how is she?

RODDY: Woman? Them different, sir.

TREVOR: (*Smirking.*) In the dog house again, are ya?

RODDY: This fellow on the platform tell me that he was goin' with a girl that just love to take licks.

TREVOR: Love to take licks?

RODDY: Love licks.

TREVOR: He's a woman-beater?

RODDY: Well, him say she used to attack him all the time, least little thing. One day him get fed up an' draw back him hand so – one backhand. (*Beat.*) Afterwards she apply the makeup. Take time to put it on, put it on good too. The man say the girl just look happy, laugh while she puttin' on eye shadow, lipstick. Him say when them make up, it was the best sex him ever have. Him say them fall in love all over again. These days I find myself thinkin' about it.

TREVOR: What, you…

RODDY: Me? No sir. Woman is just different.

There's a pause as RODDY takes in his environment.

So how's it in here?

TREVOR: You know, beds are hard, food's shit, room service terrible.

RODDY: I'm glad you can take this thing for joke.

TREVOR: Yeah, well. I'm here now, ennit.

RODDY: Huh! When you come in?

TREVOR: Dunno, about five weeks ago.

RODDY: You on remand five weeks an' it's only now we find out?

TREVOR: Thought I'd be out by now.

RODDY: So what is it this time?

TREVOR: Some rubbish.

RODDY: Some rubbish? Police come round to my house.

TREVOR: What?

RODDY: Police.

TREVOR: Round the house?

RODDY: Them come an' search up the house two days ago.

TREVOR: I never gave them your address.

RODDY: I was on earlies, leave your mother in bed sleeping. Six o'clock, about ten of them turn up, nearly give her heart attack. Woman on the phone in tears.

TREVOR: Bastards. They already searched up my yard, didn't find nothin'.

RODDY: Them come with big warrant. Bring a big dog too.

TREVOR: Yeah?

RODDY: An' you know, them lift that bloody dog up in the loft? Dog sniff sniff round, stick him nose inna everythin'.

TREVOR: Nah?

RODDY: Yeh, man, I start fret.

TREVOR laughs.

TREVOR: Shit.

RODDY: What? What?

TREVOR: When I was little ennit. Me an' my boys used to be up there stoppin' the coochie on the left hand side.

RODDY: Stop the what?

TREVOR: The coochie, dad. (*Mimes the action.*) We'd sit round the track with our eyes shut, an' this spliff goin' round in the Pullman. When it stopped, the nearest man had to draw on it.

RODDY: Jesus God! So all the time I think you up there playin' with trains, it's drugs?

TREVOR: Herbs dad, that aint drugs.

RODDY: It's drugs yes.

TREVOR: That thing grows in the ground, it's a natural substance, seen.

RODDY: Well tell that to the judge when him have my arse lock up in a police cell.

TREVOR laughs.

23

TREVOR: But na, man that's bang out of order. Probably means they went round Jenny's gaff.

RODDY: I don't hear from them.

TREVOR: What about Sheila?

RODDY: No hear from any of them, sir. Not a word.

TREVOR: I've still got some of my stuff at their yard, stereo, video an' thing, I don't want them cops fastin' with it.

RODDY: Why them would wanna fast with your stuff?

TREVOR: They can confiscate your property, ennit. Especially when it's drugs.

RODDY: Drugs?

TREVOR: With intent.

RODDY: Intent?

TREVOR: Intent to supply.

RODDY: You turn drug dealer?

TREVOR: They're saying it was in my possession, you get me.

RODDY: In your possession? What's wrong with you? How it get in your possession?

TREVOR: Dad, you're soundin' like them police.

Pause.

RODDY: Drugs. You certainly lookin' to kill her.

TREVOR: It's nothin', man.

RODDY: How you mean nothing? That woman believe in you, love you to death. An' all you do is bring her worries.

TREVOR: I don't mean to, alright.

RODDY: Whether you mean to or not you're doin' things that is causing pain. I don't know, Trevor, I really don't. You're a big man now, we shouldn't have to be worryin' about you still…

TREVOR: (*Angrily.*) I ask you to come here? I never ask you to come here lookin' for me. I can look after myself, alright.

RODDY is exasperated. There's a pause.

They stuck me in with this right mug. Cops are nickin' this junkie, right, an' this idiot jumped in their car an' drives off. Fool, there's some heavy duty horsepower under that bonnet, man… 'Bout he's goin' joyridin'. He lost control, ennit, knocked this kid over. He's up for manslaughter.

A pause.

RODDY: What I'm gonna say to her?

TREVOR: I dunno. Don't say nothin'.

RODDY: She sittin' in the car outside. How me can come in here an' don't say nothin'?

TREVOR: Just say I didn't pay my parkin' tickets, TV Licence or somethin' like that.

RODDY: TV licence? And what goin' to happen when you go to court?

TREVOR: This aint goin' court. They got no evidence, man, no witnesses, no fingerprints, nothin'. All they got is circumstantial.

RODDY: You didn't say the drugs was in your possession?

TREVOR: It was in the same place as me, but it weren't in my possession.

RODDY: Trevor…them not goin' to believe you.

TREVOR: They gotta link me with it first, aint they.

RODDY: Them find the link already.

TREVOR: C'mon, dad, all my previous aint got nothin' to do with drugs. They gotta prove that I owned it an' that I was gonna supply it.

RODDY: Lord God, Trevor…look at your mother…ten years of coming to places like this, she's fed up of it. And you promised you were gonna straighten yourself out.

TREVOR: What do you want me to say? Life aint no dream, man. It's tough out there, you get me.

RODDY: Tough? What you know about tough?

TREVOR: I know what man and man have to go through. Survival of the fittest. Have to reach the top, seen? I aint goin' down your way.

RODDY: My way?

TREVOR: It aint right, you get me, the whole system, the way things is goin' on.

RODDY: My way.

TREVOR: Yeah. Your way aint for me.

RODDY: Not goin' down my way?

TREVOR: There's your way an' my way.

RODDY: My way. What is my way?

TREVOR: Your way's your way.

RODDY: An' what's that?

TREVOR: If you can't see it, I aint gonna tell you it. Your way's your way, man.

RODDY: My way is to get up in the mornin' an' go to work.

TREVOR: My way's different.

RODDY: Your way? No job, no education, two pickney with two different woman, in an' out of jail, Lord God himself know how you survive.

TREVOR: Yeah, but at least I can look myself in the mirror an' say, 'Yeah, I aint no slave.'

RODDY: Slave? What the hell you talkin' about?

TREVOR: You're always goin' on about workin' seven days a week for peanuts, an' you get treated like shit.

RODDY: I work seven days a week for peanuts to put a roof over my head an' food on the damn table.

TREVOR: That's alright, you can do that. But as far as I see it, yeah, there's work an' work, y'get me.

RODDY: Work an' work? Prison must be good these days. Them turn you into a philosopher.

TREVOR: I can't do no job that I don't like, you get me.

RODDY: Like? What like have to do with anything? I do it because I have to do it.

TREVOR: You don't have to do nothin'. You don't have to do nothin' you don't wanna do.

RODDY: Where you gettin' all this nonsense?

TREVOR: I figured that shit out for myself. I aint like you. I can't deal with people orderin' me around, you get me.

RODDY: Well now them goin' to order you around. Them gonna tell you when to eat, when to sleep, when to piss, shit, when to wash, when you can go outside. Everythin' you want to do, a next man is goin' to tell you, not when, but if you can do it. Come talkin' about don't have to do nothin' you don't want to. What kinda' rubbish that?

A loud buzzer is heard.

Time short.

TREVOR: You were late, ennit.

RODDY: Need anything?

TREVOR: I'm alright.

RODDY: Money?

TREVOR: Na, I'm alright.

RODDY: You must need to buy your little things, soap, toothpaste…

TREVOR: It's alright. Uncle Monty come up.

RODDY: Monty?

TREVOR: Yeah, he sorted me out.

RODDY: Monty come here?

TREVOR: Yeah, the other day.

RODDY: When?

TREVOR: I dunno. Couple weeks, ten days, a week…the days just roll into each other, you get me.

RODDY: He never said.

TREVOR: Didn't he?

RODDY: You find out somebody in prison, an' don't say nothin'?

TREVOR: I dunno, maybe he aint got round to it?

RODDY: What's wrong with him? Look how long I know that man.

TREVOR: Easy dad, jus' leave me out of it, yeah.

RODDY: I don't know, sir, I just don't know.

Pause. RODDY composes himself.

You will write to us though, let us know what's goin' on?

TREVOR: You know I aint good at writin'.

RODDY: At least pick up the phone. You're allowed to make phone calls, isn't it?

TREVOR: You never ask me if I'm guilty.

RODDY: Are you?

Pause.

TREVOR: I'm troddin' up the road, yeah, when this criss Mercs draws up beside me. I look inside: I see Uncle Monty. I said, 'Raar, Uncle Monty poppin' style.' Said he'll give me a lift up town. So we're listenin' to music, chattin', you know, catchin' up, long time since I seen the geezer. We get to the bridge, stop at the red lights, an' I'm rappin' away, how's the missus, what you up to, rare rare rare. Two twos I look round an' he's like, gettin' out, 'Soon come.' I thought he'd gone to the offie, you get me. Then all of a sudden it was uuurrrgh uuurrrghh! Two car loads of Feds, 'Get out the car, get out the car, keep your hands where we can see 'em!' D11 gun cops. I'm thinkin', I aint done nothin' so I'll just play it cool. Next thing, I'm face down in the gutter, spread up, with guns all over me. I'm lyin' there an' they're tossing the motor. They open the boot an' find some major kilos of Charlie. I see all this white powder an' I think, 'Fuckin' 'ell, what's Uncle Monty goin' on with, I didn't know this was his field.' Anyway they get me down the nick. Then I find out the car's a ringer as well, an' the Blue Boys are pinning it all on me, everything.

RODDY is shocked.

RODDY: No, no, no, no…

TREVOR: (*Pause.*) You believe me, don't you dad?

RODDY: What're you trying to do, what you tryin' to do?
Believe you? Before you were even a twinkle in your
mother's eye I know that man. We eat together, live
together, down to sleepin' in the same bed, an' you can
stand there an' lie to my face like that? You're a bloody
disgrace! You should be ashamed of yourself, man. Son
of mine… Son of mine?

Exit RODDY.

Fade down lights.

Scene 3

A court anteroom.

Enter RODDY and MONTY.

MONTY: I hate this place. It's a bad luck place. I was
drivin' around lookin' for somewhere to park an' I said
to myself, 'This place is bad luck.'

MONTY sparks up a cigarette.

RODDY: What's wrong with you?

MONTY: What?

RODDY: You don't see the sign?

MONTY: Relax, man.

MONTY takes a deep pull and glances at his watch.

RODDY: You surprise me, you know.

MONTY: How you mean?

RODDY: You always surprise me.

MONTY: I surprise you?

RODDY: I'm just here wonderin'…wonderin' what wind blow you this way.

MONTY: The whirlwind, man. The whirlwind.

RODDY: You surprise me.

Pause.

MONTY: Bad luck, this place. A friend of mine get locked up here once. Bluey, you know him?

RODDY: I know Bluey.

MONTY: Long time ago. He grab a fried chicken from a chip shop. Sit down same place in the doorway an' eat it. When the shopkeeper ask for money, Bluey say, 'Tchoh, stop make noise at my head, man, you don't see me eatin'?'

They laugh.

MONTY: Yes. Him tell the judge his belly did dead fe' hungry an' tell him fe' do it.

RODDY: That's Bluey all over.

MONTY: The judge direct him to tell his belly that it goin' to prison for two weeks.

They laugh some more.

RODDY: Fe' true, man. Bluey was a funny man alright. An' him black, too.

MONTY: Bluey was black bad. The original black man. Well him gone now.

RODDY: Gone?

MONTY: Dead.

RODDY: Bluey dead?

MONTY: Bluey dead.

RODDY: When him dead?

MONTY: Dead two weeks.

RODDY: Two weeks?

MONTY: You never know 'bout it?.

RODDY: I never know 'bout it. No, sir.

MONTY: I tell you 'bout it.

RODDY: You tell me 'bout it?

MONTY: I tell your missus.

RODDY: Muriel?

MONTY: Muriel.

RODDY: No, sir.

MONTY: One big funeral, man. Horse drawn carriage, food, drink… Bwoy, black people love them food, sir…specially when somebody else pay for it. Bluey was a popular man. Him get a good send off for true.

RODDY: Bluey dead.

MONTY: (*Beat.*) There was a time not too long ago we used to just go to parties, birthdays, weddings, christenings. Now its funerals, burials, cemeteries. Looks like we reach the dead zone.

RODDY: (*Pause.*) What was his name?

MONTY: Who?

RODDY: Bluey. I figure I know the man, must be twenty years, him dead an' I don't know his real name.

MONTY: Bluey, man. Everybody know him as Bluey.

RODDY: Bluey. How old he was?

MONTY: Fifty, fifty-two, somethin' like that.

RODDY: Young man still.

MONTY: When the Big Man upstairs call, go you must.

RODDY: For true.

MONTY: Them say Bluey wake up dead. His heart give out in the night. You is what now, sixty-seven?

RODDY: Sixty-five. You're older, isn't it?

MONTY: Me? No man, I'm sixty-four.

RODDY: From which part? You is seventy. At least that.

MONTY: G'weh! Me younger than you, man. I'm little more than sixty-four.

RODDY: You must be the first man reach retirement an' the years turn back, start to rewind.

MONTY: After you just jealous cos me younger, better lookin' an' fitter than you. See it here…

MONTY sings and dances to Prince Buster's Ska tune, 'Madness'.

(*Singing.*) Madness, Madness
They call it madness…

RODDY: Monty, watch yourself.

MONTY: (*Continuing.*) Madness, Madness
They call it madness…

RODDY: Be careful, you know, man.

MONTY: (*Continuing.*) You got to be rougher
You got to be tougher
Madness, Madness
They call it gladness.

*The dancing ends in a huff and puff. MONTY mops his
brow.*

Whooh! You see them moves, there? So the girls them
used to queue up, man…used to wet up themselves to get
on the dancefloor with me.

RODDY: Mind you take your boasty self wind an' grind so
them have to carry you outa' here on one foot.

MONTY: Stamina, man, plenty stamina. I bet you wan'
know my secret.

RODDY: Secret? What secret?

MONTY: Blood.

RODDY: Blood?

MONTY: A quart of blood every week. I prefer the heifer,
'cos them young still, fresh.

RODDY: Cow's blood?

MONTY: Yeah, man.

RODDY: You drink cow's blood?

MONTY: Drink it yes.

RODDY: Lord God, the man turn vampire!

MONTY: A friend of mine, Hamed, is a halal butcher.
Before them can eat the meat them must drain the blood.
I can get some for you, y'know.

RODDY: You crazy?

MONTY: It's safe, man. All the top sportsman an' film star
is doin' it.

RODDY: You don't hear about mad cow disease?

MONTY: Nothin' wrong with British beef, man.

RODDY: That's what them tell you.

MONTY: I eat it all the time.

RODDY: You see what I mean.

MONTY: Hamed say Scottish beef is the best because disease can't flourish inna them cold temperature.

RODDY: Monty, you alright? You sure all that cow's blood not turnin' you fool-fool?

MONTY: You can laugh. But when you dead an' gone, me still here about.

RODDY: Well, I'm not dead yet.

MONTY pulls a flask from his jacket pocket and swigs. He offers a drink to RODDY who takes a little sip.

MONTY: White rum… Overproof.

There's a pause.

RODDY: Monty…

MONTY: What?

RODDY: Trevor…

MONTY: What?

RODDY: That night…

MONTY: What?

RODDY: That night, in that car, the night Trevor got picked up by police…

MONTY: What?

RODDY: You were drivin' that car.

MONTY: What me? What, you think… Me?

RODDY: I know you were at the wheel that night.

MONTY: That night? No, no, man, me? No sir, not me. I…
I… Not, not me.

Another pause.

RODDY: I don't understand, you know, how we ever get to
this? I'm lookin' at this thing here an'…it's…this is…this
whole thing is just…it's a fuckin' mess.

MONTY: I know.

RODDY: To tell you the truth, I don't know how I'm goin'
to deal with it.

MONTY: You just deal with it.

RODDY: Deal with it? A man's life is at stake here. A man's
life!

Pause.

MONTY: The way I see it, it will sort itself out.

RODDY: It will sort itself out?

MONTY: Yeah, man, these things always do.

RODDY: You see you?

MONTY: What, me?

RODDY: You!

MONTY: Roddy, man…

RODDY: This, all of this is down to you.

MONTY: Me?

*RODDY explodes, aggressively grabbing MONTY by the lapels.
A scuffle ensues.*

RODDY: You bastard…takin' me for a fuckin' fool!

MONTY: Wha' you doin'?

RODDY: Everythin' you do is rotten…

MONTY: Ease up, man!

RODDY: It's jus' trouble, trouble!

MONTY: Blood claat – Is fight you wan' fight me?

RODDY: From I know you it's nothin' but worries, man, worries…

MONTY shakes RODDY loose.

MONTY: Get your fuckin' hands off me!

RODDY pulls back from the brink and releases MONTY. There's a pause as they straighten their clothing.

Look here, man, I know you blame me for this bullshit.

RODDY: I'm to blame somebody else?

MONTY: You wanna check yourself.

RODDY: What?

MONTY: You need to look in the mirror.

RODDY: I must look in the mirror?

MONTY: He's confused, the boy's confused. Don't know if he's comin' or goin'.

RODDY: What am I hearin' here?

MONTY: You confuse him, man.

RODDY: I teach him right from wrong. What you did is wrong.

MONTY: Wrong? Huh!

RODDY: You're a selfish man, you know that.

MONTY: Yes, I'm selfish. I look after number one. But you…you go on like…

37

RODDY: Me what?

MONTY: Nothin' man.

RODDY: No, go on, say it, say it.

MONTY: Any black man with sense would know to scatter. Gone!

RODDY: What you mean? I don't understand you. What you talkin' about?

MONTY: That boy sit down there thinkin' all the bullshit you put in his head all these years.

RODDY: No, man, you talkin' stupid.

MONTY: Whether a man innocent or guilty, a black man is guilty by virtue of the colour of his skin. I learn that a long time ago. That's how the white man see it. That's how it stay.

RODDY: You're wrong, man. You're wrong. I tell you you're wrong. You is wrong. Wrong.

A brooding pause.

MONTY: So how long you know?

RODDY: I'm his father. Don't you forget that.

MONTY: (*Pause.*) Look here, Roddy, it was a accident, man.

RODDY: Accident?

MONTY: The thing just happen.

RODDY: The thing just happen an' you couldn't tell me? You couldn't come to me an' tell me my son, your godson, get arrested?

MONTY: You talkin' like I wanted him to get arrested.

RODDY: My mind would think so.

MONTY: What you sayin'?

RODDY: I'm sayin', Monty, this time you gone too far.

MONTY: Tchoh. You worry too much, man. The boy's alright, he can take care of himself. He knows how things work at street level. Strong seed, y'see. I sow the seed, you tend the crop and we reap the harvest. He's just like me, man. Like father like son. He's a player, jus' like his ol' man...

A commotion off.

TREVOR: (*Off.*) Alright mate, alright...this is the family waiting room, you wanna come in with me? Fuck's sake...

Enter TREVOR.

(*On.*) Like a puppy on a fuckin' lead, them mans followin' me everywhere.

RODDY: What you expect, you're on trial.

TREVOR: I aint guilty, I'm innocent, I'm a free man still. I can't even take a piss without them guards standin' over me.

TREVOR sees MONTY.

Uncle Monty!

MONTY: Wha' appen Trevor...

TREVOR and MONTY hug each other.

TREVOR: I knew you'd come. Nice one, man. Appreciate it.

MONTY: You alright?

TREVOR: Yeah, it's alright.

MONTY: So how's things?

TREVOR: Just been chattin' to my brief, there's a bit of a hold up. They're runnin' late.

MONTY: So what time it start?

TREVOR: Dunno, you know...half hour, hour, they might not even go on today.

MONTY: Tchoh!

MONTY glances at his watch.

TREVOR: Wassup?

MONTY: I'm on a meter round the corner. I'm gonna move the car. Soon come, yeah.

TREVOR: Yeah, no probs.

MONTY: Soon come.

Exit MONTY.

TREVOR: Good of him to show up here.

RODDY: Good of him – ?

TREVOR: Give him some props, dad. Most man would be nowhere to be seen.

RODDY: Cheek of the man.

Pause.

TREVOR: You get my letter?

RODDY: What?

TREVOR: My last letter, you get it?

RODDY: Which one?

TREVOR: Sent it to mum. I was after my pastels.

RODDY: You never get them?

TREVOR: Nothin' come. I even asked the governor.

RODDY: She never send them?

TREVOR: No, or I wouldn't be asking.

RODDY: You was good at drawing, ennit. Teacher said you had real talent. Remember that competition you win, get your picture in the paper?

TREVOR: Dad, I was eight.

RODDY: It's a pity you didn't keep it up. (*Beat.*) She never send – we even talked about the bloody thing… Spend all her time singin' an' clappin' at bloody church…what's this woman goin' on with?

TREVOR: You two, man.

RODDY: After a while them get funny, you know, quarrel, love to quarrel. You lucky you not married. You stand same place here, an' hear the chatter chatter.

Pause.

TREVOR: What's she sayin'…about all this?

RODDY: Nothin' much.

TREVOR: Nothing?

RODDY: Well, she… I dunno…things are rough, right now, it's kinda' difficult. We're not speakin'.

TREVOR: Not speaking? Why, what…

RODDY: Aah, y'know, it's nothin', just one of them things.

TREVOR: (*Pause.*) It's because of me, ennit?

RODDY: You? No man.

TREVOR: It is. It's cos I'm here. She can't handle it.

RODDY: Don't think like that. It's not you.

TREVOR: She's not here, is she? It's the first day of my friggin' trial an' she aint here.

RODDY: She…

TREVOR: Where is she, where is she, dad?

RODDY: (*Beat.*) It's a long time we been married, y'know. Sometimes people just drift apart, no particular reason. Just one of them things. We'll be alright. We'll get by.

TREVOR: Before I forget…

TREVOR produces a rolled up chalk drawing, a portrait of a stern old woman.

RODDY: What's this? You do this?

TREVOR: It's not rightly finished.

RODDY: Look at that…

TREVOR: Never had pastels so I had to borrow the chalks.

RODDY: You see, see how much talent you have? You're talented, got talent, talented.

TREVOR: You like it?

There's a pause while RODDY scrutinises the drawing.

RODDY: Who is it, your mother?

TREVOR: No. No-one.

RODDY: You couldn't put a smile on it?

TREVOR: You don't have to have it.

RODDY: I want it.

TREVOR: I did it for you. For mum.

RODDY: Thanks son. (*Hugs TREVOR.*) I was thinkin' about that programme on the telly.

TREVOR: Which programme?

RODDY: What's it called now, Crimestoppers?

TREVOR: Crimestoppers?

RODDY: Kinda' police show.

TREVOR: I know what it is.

RODDY: I was thinkin' that…

TREVOR: What?

RODDY: You don't have to know about it.

TREVOR: Dad, what you sayin'?

RODDY: What if, God forbid, they find you guilty?

TREVOR: They won't.

RODDY: You so sure about that?

TREVOR: I aint goin' nowhere.

RODDY: What a way you confident.

TREVOR: It's gonna be alright.

RODDY: (*Pause.*) Look, you don't even have to give your name or anything. I can do it, anonymous like.

TREVOR: Anonymous like what?

RODDY: Anonymous like, Trevor Charles is innocent. The man you're lookin' for is Montgomery Griffiths.

TREVOR: You'd do that?

RODDY: You're my son.

TREVOR: You two go way back. You've known each other for years.

RODDY: You're my son.

TREVOR: (*Pause.*) I said I thumbed a lift from some white man…

RODDY: They'll understand.

TREVOR: They'd have to release me.

RODDY: That's right.

TREVOR: (*Enjoying the moment.*) Get release…get off scot-free. It'd be like I was laughin' at them all along… Laugh at them, yes.

RODDY: You see it now.

TREVOR: (*Beat.*) Nah, nah, they don't like me, man. They'll do me for somethin', wastin' police time, obstruction, somethin' like that. The feds don't like me an' I don't like them.

RODDY: Why would they do that when they have the right man?

TREVOR: (*Pause.*) So what you're saying is you go to some phonebox somewhere…it'll have to be one outa' town…

RODDY: Simple as that. It's up to you now, Trevor.

TREVOR moves across the room, contemplating.

RODDY: (*Beat.*) That number, what's the number again now, it's O800 44 55 somethin'…?

TREVOR: No…

RODDY: It's somethin' like that.

TREVOR: No…

RODDY: Maybe it's 55 44…? I'll ring directory enquiries…

TREVOR stops RODDY.

TREVOR: No, they'll know it's me.

RODDY: Nothin' of the sort, man.

TREVOR: This aint television, dad. It don't matter if I'm inside or outside. They'll put two an' two together, game over.

RODDY: So you gonna give up just like that? You're a family man, Trevor, with a young family. You just gonna turn your back on them, let other people decide what happen to you?

TREVOR: I aint no grass, dad, I aint no informer. I do what you say, it won't matter if I'm in or out, I'd be a grass. And d'you know what happens to grasses?

TREVOR moves across the room.

RODDY: (*Pause.*) Mr Cummins tell you to speak slow when you get up there?

TREVOR: I aint goin' up there.

RODDY: What?

TREVOR: I don't have to.

RODDY: You have to go up there.

TREVOR: Cummins says I don't.

RODDY: Cummins? What's this? I don't believe what I'm hearin'.

TREVOR: He reckons they got no case an' it's up to them to prove me guilty.

RODDY: No man, I don't agree with that. Where is this man?

TREVOR: He knows what he's doin'.

RODDY: You don't see that him an' all of them, defence an' prosecution is friend-friend, work colleagues. It's a game to them, it don't bother them if you get lock up.

TREVOR: Dad, remind me when it was you took the bar exam?

RODDY: A man accuse you of somethin' you never do an' you don't defend yourself? Whoever hear that? I'm gonna talk to that man.

TREVOR: (*Snapping.*) I told you not to.

RODDY: I just gonna find out –

TREVOR: – What's wrong with you, interfering? Don't fuck me around, dad, don't fuck me about. This is… You'll… (*Beat.*) Jus' keep outa' my shit, alright.

Pause. RODDY moves over towards the door and peeps out as MONTY passes him, entering.

RODDY: (*Incredulous.*) The man say him not goin' on the stand.

MONTY: What's this?

TREVOR: Nothin'. He's jus' goin' on all freaky deaky cos I ain't givin' evidence.

MONTY: Your man advise you that?

TREVOR: He knows what he's doing, y'get me?

MONTY: He's right, y'know. Them bloody QC's good to use trickery and fancy words to turn a black man inside out.

TREVOR: I know, that's why I'm chillin'.

MONTY: Good. Look confident, you'll do alright. C'mon, cheer up, man.

RODDY turns back into the room.

RODDY: Trevor, you couldn't put on a suit this mornin'?

MONTY: Your man's gonna destroy the prosecution.

RODDY: Come to court without a suit…

MONTY: See the prosecution man face? Favour mash mango.

MONTY and TREVOR laugh.

RODDY: Not gonna take the stand, Lord have mercy.

MONTY: Them little small men always extra loud, y'know, extra tough…

RODDY: You can't give them ammunition…

MONTY: Always have to face him down, look him in the eye…

MONTY stoops with his joke. TREVOR laughs heartily.

RODDY: You have to change the way they look at you…

MONTY: Them little man is jus' plain extra.

RODDY: I coulda' brought a suit for you.

TREVOR: I don't like suits.

RODDY: You don't have to like the suit. You just have to wear it.

TREVOR: Hear what, I see rapists an' paedophiles on the fraggle wing goin' court every day, wearin' nice suits, lookin' sharp. They're still rapists an' paedophiles. A suit ain't gonna change that.

RODDY: But them look smart. They walk street an' nobody know what they do.

TREVOR: A suit is just a mask.

RODDY: We all have to wear masks sometimes.

TREVOR: Look, dad, fuck the suit!

RODDY: Trevor!

TREVOR: No, if they're gonna lock me up, they're gonna lock me up.

RODDY: At least go down fighting.

TREVOR: Why you pickin' on me, why you always pickin' on me?

RODDY: I'm pickin' on you?

TREVOR: Always pickin' on me, distressing me like you begrudge me, like I owe you somethin'.

RODDY: Owe me somethin'?

MONTY: Roddy, you upsettin' the boy.

RODDY: I'm tryin' to help him.

TREVOR: Help me? How you gonna help me? When I needed help where was you?

RODDY: I ever refuse to help you?

TREVOR: Yes.

RODDY: When, when?

MONTY: Roddy!

RODDY: I try to bring you up right. Everythin' that a man do for his children I do for you. An' look what I get in return.

TREVOR: Shouldn't bother then should ya.

RODDY: Look at this, look at this…

MONTY: Alright the two of you. This is family. We look after each other, support each other. C'mon!

TREVOR: Alright, alright…

An intercom crackles an announcement.

INTERCOM: Court fourteen, The Crown versus Trevor Charles…

TREVOR: This is it.

MONTY throws an arm over TREVOR's shoulder.

MONTY: Good luck.

TREVOR and RODDY grunt at each other.

Exit TREVOR.

Fade down lights.

Scene 4

The court anteroom.

MONTY enters with an arm slung round TREVOR's shoulders.

MONTY: That wasn't too bad. Your man, whatsisname, Cummins? Might consider using him myself one of these days. He's alright.

TREVOR: It was bad, man.

MONTY: Coulda' been worse.

TREVOR: Couldn't be worse. Standin' up there with them chattin' you like that, linkin' you with all that drugs an' other shit. How does it look when I got kids? I see the jury, the way they looked at me.

MONTY: At least that's out the way now. Just the judge's summin' up to come.

TREVOR: I'm goin' down, you know. I can feel it.

MONTY: Don't think like that.

TREVOR: You heard what the man said.

MONTY: I heard him say, 'If there's the slightest doubt in your mind, it's your duty to acquit.' There's a whole heap of doubts in this case. Remember that.

TREVOR: Yeah, you're right.

MONTY: Yeah man, it will work out, trust me. As long as you righteous in here an' hold tight, you will come through.

TREVOR: (*Pause.*) It's weird but at one point in there I wanted to laugh, you know. That's fucked up, man, I'm starin' down the barrel of a category A Bird an' I wanna laugh. I started thinkin' about the time – you told me about Kingston Harbour, how you used to watch them ships comin' an' goin'… I laugh…

MONTY: Yes sir, three o'clock every Tuesday. Used to see all the women bawlin' their eyes out. I ask the harbour master, 'Where all these men goin'.' The man laugh, 'What do you bwoy? You stupid?'

TREVOR joins in the last part of the story with MONTY.

TREVOR / MONTY: 'Them goin' to Englan'. You no hear say the streets of London paved with gold?'

They laugh.

TREVOR: I don't know how you lot managed that boat business though.

MONTY: Me travel them way there by boat? No, sir, I travel in style. I fly into this country.

TREVOR: Yeah?

MONTY: The only black man on that plane was me. Pretty air hostess servin' me whiskey like I was somebody.

TREVOR: That's fuckin' wicked, y'get me.

MONTY breaks into a ream of cackling laughter.

MONTY: Three years I watch those men, dress up in their
fine suit, walk that plank, leave them wife wavin' at the
dockside, 'Don't worry darlin', I will send for you. I will
send money back for you to buy a ticket to Englan'.'
(*Beat.*) Huh, I cast my line, hook one of them economic
widows. An' it's her husband pay for my first class ticket
to England.

They laugh.

MONTY: I was a rude bwoy them times.

TREVOR: Rude boy for true, Uncle.

MONTY: Yeah, man. (*Pause.*) You know somethin', know
what I'm gonna do? I'm gonna make it up to you,
y'know. I'm gonna sort you out proper, slide some
dollars your way, throw in a little holiday...Jamaica.

TREVOR: Jamaica? No, no...

MONTY: White rum, sunshine, girls...

TREVOR: No, no, no...

MONTY: An' you know how Jamaican girls love a
Englishman.

TREVOR: I don't want it.

MONTY: Alright, where you wanna go?

TREVOR: Nowhere.

MONTY: Anywhere, man? Anywhere you wanna go in the
world. America, Africa, Russia, even China.

TREVOR: No.

MONTY: You ever hear about the Great Wall of China?
You can see that thing from space, y'know?

TREVOR: No.

MONTY: F'true, man, one of the Seven Wonders of the World...

TREVOR: No...

MONTY: Like them pyramids in Egypt. It's black man build them things, y'know. Yeah, man, when white man livin' in a hole in the ground, black man a' read the stars.

TREVOR: You don't hear me, no.

MONTY: No? The man refuse Jamaica! How a man can refuse Jamaica? That is the paradise island, y'know.

TREVOR: I don't wanna go nowhere.

MONTY: You don't want to go nowhere?

TREVOR: I'll stay where I am.

MONTY: You don't want a holiday?

TREVOR: No.

MONTY: That's alright. I know you is a family man.

TREVOR: It aint like that.

MONTY: No worries, man. I'll give you the money. You can do whatever you want with it.

TREVOR: No.

MONTY: So what you want?

TREVOR: I don't want nothin'.

MONTY: So what...you don't want nothin'?

TREVOR: Nothin'.

MONTY: Nothing?

TREVOR: Yeah, nothing.

MONTY: C'mon, man...

TREVOR: Nothin'. No more. It's over, man.

MONTY: (*Pause.*) Over? What's over?

TREVOR: I'm... I'm done with it.

MONTY: Done with what?

TREVOR: Look, I aint gonna grass or anythin' like that but...

MONTY is concerned more than ever before, and it shows.

MONTY: Grass?

TREVOR: I know the runnings...

MONTY: Who said anythin' about grass?

TREVOR: I just don't wanna get involved no more.

MONTY: You already involved.

TREVOR: But no more.

MONTY: So what, you talk to somebody?

TREVOR: I'm talkin' to you, man.

MONTY: Who you talk to?

TREVOR: See, you aint even listenin' to me.

MONTY: I'm hearin' you, man...

TREVOR: You think I don't know you just show up here to make sure I don't drop you in it.

MONTY: Trevor listen, man, this thing...you an' me, the two of we...

TREVOR: I been thinkin' about it.

MONTY: We in the same situation...

TREVOR: I'm supposed to be your blood!

MONTY: (*Sternly.*) Shut up, man! Shut up! What's wrong with you? Just shut up. You think this is just trouble for me? For you? No, sir, other people involved inna this thing, heavy people, you understand. People you don't fuck with. Not even police fuck with these people.

TREVOR: Fuckin' 'ell...

MONTY: (*Pause.*) Man fuck with these guys, end up on the missin' persons list. Two twos body surface on the river, float on the downstream, head, hands, foot, gone. No identification. Years before them find out who you is. By then nobody care. To these fuckers life is cheap.

TREVOR: You're mixing with mans like that an' you've stuck me bang in the middle of 'em.

Pause.

MONTY: I wasn't gonna say nothin' but things have changed.

TREVOR: Changed?

MONTY: It's gettin' hot out there. Man an' man is gettin' queasy.

TREVOR: Queasy? Whaddya mean?

MONTY: Every day, messages on my phone, my tyres slashed, even petrol they pour in my letterbox...

TREVOR: Oh, man...

MONTY: They're warning me...

TREVOR: Warning you? Why, why's that?

MONTY: They don't trust you, me, us...

TREVOR: Me? They don't even know me. There's only one thing linking them to me... (*A beat, realisation.*) an' that's you. It don't matter jack what I say, cos I don't know who the fuck they are. This is about you. You're protectin' your own skin.

MONTY: No, no man, this is a two horse race.

TREVOR: I'm blood. You're supposed to look out for me.

MONTY: I'm lookin' out for you, believe.

TREVOR: You couldn't give a red cent tuppenny fuck about me.

MONTY: That aint true, man, I'm your father.

TREVOR: You might be my father but you aint my dad.

MONTY: Trevor…

TREVOR: Don't come to me with that.

MONTY: Alright, so a next man brought you up. But as sure as the sun rise in the east, you an' me is one blood.

TREVOR: Bad blood.

MONTY: Trevor…

TREVOR: No, man, no…

MONTY: I was there, man. I never interfered but I was there.

TREVOR: And what, so I owe you somethin' now? I must give up all my shit for you?

MONTY: Don't look at it like that, man.

TREVOR: You aint my dad, alright!

MONTY: What you gonna do, Trevor? You gonna give me up? You gonna call my name? (*Beat.*) Well alright, go on, you do what you have to do. There's the door. Go on, go on, tell them. Go ahead.

TREVOR: (*Pause.*) You aint my dad.

MONTY: Trevor, I might not be what you expect, but blood is thicker than water. You're my son, an' I love you...

TREVOR: (*Beat.*) Lets get it straight, right...we got no beef, yeah?

MONTY: You want me to beg?

TREVOR: No beef between us, yeah?

MONTY: That what you want?

TREVOR: No beef between us, right?

MONTY: Alright, here I am, I'm beggin' you, Trevor please... I'm begging you.

TREVOR: No beef?

MONTY: Beef?

TREVOR: Beef. We got no beef, no beef...

MONTY: No beef.

TREVOR: Right, now we're clear. Don't come round me no more.

MONTY: Don't go on like that, man.

TREVOR: I mean it! Just keep the fuck away from me!

Exit TREVOR.

MONTY: Trevor, Trevor, please...please.

Fade down lights.

Scene 5

The court anteroom.

Enter RODDY, man-handling MONTY into the room.

MONTY: Wha'...what is it, what's goin' on?

RODDY: Where you goin'?

MONTY: What?

RODDY: I see you.

MONTY: See me what?

RODDY: I see you shufflin' off.

MONTY: What?

RODDY: The verdict was announced an' I see you...

MONTY: See me what?

RODDY: I see you soft shoe shuffle outa' the court like, like...like a rat...

MONTY: What you talkin' about?

RODDY: Deserting a sinking ship.

MONTY: Eh?

RODDY: Where you goin' in such a hurry?

MONTY: Hurry? No, man...

RODDY: I run to catch you.

MONTY: No, man, I just can't believe it. I just wanna get out of that room, with them people. I can't believe... They did it. In an hour.

RODDY: Less than an hour.

MONTY: All of them?

RODDY: Unanimous.

MONTY: What a jury blood claat bad mind.

RODDY: They found him guilty, Monty, guilty!

MONTY: All them see is black. If it was a white boy it wouldn't get this far much less.

RODDY: I warn him. I warned him.

MONTY: It's them against us, man. Always against us.

RODDY: But you must defend yourself. You don't get up there an' defend yourself, the jury must believe you guilty.

MONTY: He must appeal that verdict.

RODDY: He can't appeal, he can't appeal.

MONTY: How you mean? It's his right to appeal.

RODDY: If he had stood up there an' put his case he'd have somethin' to appeal against.

MONTY: That don't matter a raas to them.

RODDY: They catch him in a stolen car full up with drugs. In a stolen car full of drugs, with black skin, an' in court without a suit.

MONTY: Suit?

RODDY: They respect the suit. The suit is responsibility, society, order. The suit is the system. They believe the suit. They would believe that suit more than anything he could say.

MONTY: That judge practically direct the jury to find him guilty.

RODDY: He's not guilty, Monty. Tell them, tell them he's not guilty.

MONTY: They know he's not guilty. They don't need me to tell them that.

RODDY: How did I let this go so far?

MONTY: The boy's bad lucky.

RODDY: Bad lucky?

MONTY: He was in the wrong place at the wrong time.

RODDY: Wrong place wrong time?

MONTY: A man stop to give you a lift an' you end up in jail?

RODDY: Well it certainly turn out to be the wrong place right time for you.

MONTY: So it seems.

RODDY: If it was down to me, a next man would be in chains right now.

MONTY: Roddy, don't go on them ways.

RODDY: I sat there an' watched you let that boy go down for you.

MONTY: I'm sorry man, I'm really sorry.

RODDY: It's like I been servin' a sentence, holdin' onto this thing, sayin' nothin', down to not even tellin' my wife. How she gonna handle this when she find out?

MONTY: Hold tight, man, calm it down.

RODDY: I'm sick an' tired of people takin' the piss out of me, lookin' at me like I'm some sort of bystander. I'm not a blasted bystander. That's my son they just locked up, my son.

MONTY: Your son?

RODDY: What, you the father now? You supply the juice? You think you is the man because you take up yourself an' fuck my wife?

RODDY is upset, tearful, collapsing with exasperation.

I loved her, man! I loved her.

MONTY: Roddy…

MONTY catches hold of RODDY.

RODDY: I know what I should have done and didn't do it. I'm to blame for this, it's my fault.

MONTY: Don't blame yourself, man, it's not you.

RODDY: She waits, you know...yes, she can't bring herself to come here, so she waits in a church, talks to a bloody priest all day...til I come home an' tell her this an' that, anything but the truth. What do I do now?

MONTY: Roddy, we come through bigger than this, right?

RODDY: Her only child is in prison for something he didn't do an' I can't tell her why. As far as she's concerned, I walked him down the aisle to wickedness.

MONTY: We have to stick together, support each other.

RODDY: Twenty odd years...I can't do it no more. I can't... Can't...

MONTY: Believe me when I tell you that Trevor goin' to prison was the only way.

RODDY: The only way!

MONTY: Not even you would recognise him if they did get hold of him. These people, they're dangerous, man. They don't take risks. Right now prison is the best place for him.

RODDY: Hit me. Go on, hit me... Lick me, down, man!

MONTY: Quiet Roddy...

RODDY: (*Yelling.*) Hit me! Kill me! I want you to kill me!

MONTY: Roddy, no...hold it down...

RODDY: Do it, do it, man! I want you to do it...

MONTY: There's people about... Let's go outside...we'll sort it outside...

MONTY leads a forlorn RODDY out of the room.

Fade down lights.

Scene 6

A dreary bedsit. The top attic room of a heavily converted and populated Victorian house.

Wallpaper peels off the walls in places and damp patches are evident. Prints of trains hang on the walls. A British Rail uniform hangs on a hook by the door, it seems to dominate the room. There's a model train track set up on the floor.

A RADIO is playing. A new model train engine is running round the track. After a moment RODDY stops the train running, picks it up and sits at a table to work on it.

RADIO: A little bit of bunching early on, after a clean start on this gloriously sunny day, with Gary Stone on Johnny Be Good at seven to two leading the three forty-five one mile Champions Chase Stake by a nose from Daffy's Glory at six to one, Aden Cox, the rider there. Then it's Soldier Boy, the two to one favourite ridden by Danny McGuire, followed by Royal Betty at thirty-three to one with Jim Cannon in the seat…

RODDY: Come on!

RADIO: Danny Biff in the blue on Hoseason and the blindfolded Little Lord ridden by Mick Carini both come in at sixteens bringing up the rear…

RODDY: Come on Betty!

RADIO: Things look to be hotting up nicely two furlongs out, with Johnny Be Good being pushed a little by Soldier boy and Daffy's Glory. Royal Betty's closing fast on the rails, with a small gap opening up as Hoseason and Little Lord fall back.…

RODDY: Stay in there girl!

There's some banging on a wall from a neighbour.

RADIO: Royal Betty stretching out now, moving up into second behind Johnny Be Good from Soldier Boy steadily fading, as the front two take up the pace…

RODDY: Come on! Come on Elizabeth!

RADIO: They're neck and neck in the straight coming up to the finish. It's a two horse race between Royal Betty just nosing in front from Johnny Be Good. Soldier Boy's making a late dash but I don't think he's going to make an impression as Jim Cannon on Royal Betty surges away from Johnny Be Good now on the whip.

RODDY: Yes, yes…go on!

RADIO: It's tight, tight, tight as they come four lengths out in this marvellous race. But the extra stride belongs to Royal Betty as she wins the Champions Chase Stake by a nose from Johnny Be Good. A full length behind comes Soldier Boy by a stride from Daffy's Glory. Hoseason and Little Lord cantering over the line are the slow finishers.

RODDY: Yes, yes, yesssss!

RODDY throws up his arms in victory. There's more banging on the wall.

RADIO: So, the result then of the three forty-five one mile Champions Chase Stake at Kempton Park sponsored by Bic Razors with a first prize of seventeen and a half thousand pounds was first, Royal Betty at thirty-three to one. Second Johnny Be Good seven to two. Third Soldier Boy the two to one favourite. Number fourteen Wakers Dressing Gown was a non runner.

There's some aggressive banging from the neigbouring flat.

Jim Cannon bags his second winner of the afternoon from what can only be described as a shaky start on Royal Betty, a young filly with a not unknown reputation for nervous starts…

RODDY switches off the radio.

RODDY: Hush up man! It's alright for you playin' your jiggy jiggy music til all hours. I'm on a winnin' streak here, man.

There's a knock at the door. RODDY grabs a broom.

I'm not alone in here. My son is here with me. He's over six foot tall, so you don't want to mess around with me. You hear?

The door knocks again.

TREVOR: (*Off.*) Dad, it's me, open the door.

RODDY: Trevor!

RODDY replaces the broom and exits.

Momentarily MONTY enters.

MONTY: That's a bitch piece of stairs…

TREVOR enters followed by RODDY.

I was jus' sayin' that's a bitch piece of stairs you got there.

TREVOR: Halfway up you was in real trouble, ennit, uncle?

MONTY: Wha' you talkin' 'bout? All you young boys have nothin' on me.

TREVOR: Oh yeah?

MONTY: I'm as fit as a fiddle. Wan' me to go down? I'll show you, y'know.

TREVOR: Go on, then.

MONTY: Tchoh! I can't be bothered.

TREVOR: You're full of it, mate.

MONTY: It's test you wan' test me?

MONTY drops to the floor and starts a press-up routine.

RODDY: Monty, get up, man.

MONTY: Hold on…two, three, four…

TREVOR shows off his new clothes.

TREVOR: What do you think of my new garms, dad?

RODDY: How you gonna live if you spend off all your relief money already?

TREVOR: No, I aint. I stepped outa' that jail this morning, an' there was Uncle Monty.

RODDY: He knew you was comin' out today?

TREVOR: I was glad to see him still, you get me. Cos that train journey is long, dread. Look, he sorted me out with these threads. They're the dog's, man, look at the cut.

MONTY: …nineteen, twenty. Whooh!

MONTY gets to his feet and mops his brow.

TREVOR: That was never twenty.

MONTY: Twenty, yes.

TREVOR: Check him, he's a joker, ennit. You're a joker, uncle.

MONTY lights a smoke.

RODDY: Congratulations on the parole.

TREVOR: Believe! Man maintains he aint guilty usually means the full hundred, f'real.

RODDY: You must be doin' somethin' right.

TREVOR: I dunno y'know, cos them psycho-parole geezers are the original racists. But I aint complainin' still, you get me.

RODDY: You look different, bigger.

TREVOR: All that iron I been pumpin'. They got a well tasty gym up there.

RODDY: You're becomin' a man, fillin' out. You see your boys?

TREVOR: Check this, a couple months back both babymothers' were up on a visit, same time. I hadta' do a bit of shufflin' to balance it out so they didn't buck up in there, or it woulda' been bare worries in the dance, you get me.

RODDY: Trevor, you still goin' on with them foolishness?

TREVOR: Man, I was runnin' from one room to the other, 'Yeah, yeah, what's happenin'? Cool, cool, alright, baby, alright… Soon come, yeah.' Then in the other room, 'Thanks for comin', yeah. How ya doin'? Alright…' Kiss kiss. 'Alright little youth…look, I got somethin' goin' on, back in five, yeah.' It was crazy, believe. The woman them was, 'What's wrong with you? What's wrong with you? I come all this way an' you goin' on dark, ennit…' It was coarse, dread.

RODDY: (*Exasperated.*) Oh, I don't know.

TREVOR: (*Pause.*) Kids grow so quick when you aint around. Nex' thing, them geezers gonna be walkin' street. (*Scans the room.*) Just the one room?

RODDY: Toilet, shower through there.

TREVOR: There's no telly.

RODDY: (*Glancing at MONTY.*) No smoking either.

TREVOR: Even in the jailhouse you can smoke an' watch TV.

RODDY: Well, this ain't no jailhouse, remember that.

Pause. RODDY and MONTY speak simultaneously.

RODDY / MONTY: So what –

MONTY: Go on.

RODDY: No, you go.

MONTY: I wasn't sayin' nothin'. Go on, man.

RODDY: I was…sayin' nothin' really.

There's an uncomfortable air.

You look well, Monty.

MONTY: (*Modestly.*) I'm alright, man, alright. You look like you're losin' weight. You losin' weight?

RODDY: Them stairs keeps me fit. Let me get some tea together?

TREVOR: Nice one, pops.

MONTY: You have anythin' stronger?

RODDY: Coffee.

MONTY: No rum, beer?

RODDY moves towards the kitchen area and makes tea. MONTY offers TREVOR a cigarette.

Want one of these?

TREVOR: Na, mate. My body's a temple. No impurities goin' in there, f'real.

MONTY gets out a flask and offers TREVOR a drink.

What's that?

MONTY: Have a sip.

TREVOR: Alcohol?

MONTY: Rum.

TREVOR: Aah, fuck it, go on then.

TREVOR takes a slug.

RODDY peers out through the tiny window by the kitchen sink.

RODDY: Tiger, here Tiger!

MONTY moves over to a sideboard and scrutinises some model train parts in a variety of boxes.

RODDY returns with a cup of tea for TREVOR.

Stupid cat sleepin' on the Chinaman roof. That's a dangerous place to sleep, y'know. Them Chinaman will eat anythin'. Two sugars, ennit?

TREVOR: Respect. So, what's happenin' in the land of dad?

RODDY: What?

TREVOR: You alright?

RODDY: Me, I'm fine. Fine.

TREVOR: Heard from mum recently?

RODDY shoots a glance at MONTY rifling through the tiny train engine parts.

RODDY: Hey, don't mess up my things, you know. I lay them all out correctly.

MONTY: Just lookin', man.

RODDY works on his model train.

RODDY: Things got a bit hectic.

TREVOR: So I hear.

RODDY: It's not easy livin' in a house full of fire an' brimstone.

TREVOR: F'real, that bible bullshit can drive a man to do anything.

RODDY: Well, she get the house, ennit.

TREVOR: Yeah, for real. Man beat a woman, that's a big payoff he's gotta suffer, y'get me.

RODDY: Beat? Who tell you – ? (*Turning to MONTY.*) What's wrong with you?

MONTY: Who me?

RODDY: Yes, you.

MONTY: I'm just havin' a look, man.

RODDY: You determined to destroy me, ennit?

MONTY: What, I can't look at these things?

RODDY: Why you tell Trevor I beat his mother?

MONTY: Well…

RODDY: Well, nothin', man. You is out of order.

MONTY: You never beat her?

RODDY: I beat her?

MONTY: Then why she throw you out?

RODDY: She throw me out? I leave.

MONTY: You leave?

RODDY: I leave.

MONTY: Maybe I get it wrong.

RODDY: Maybe 'you' wrong.

RODDY sets the train on the track. MONTY joins them.

MONTY: You never beat her?

RODDY: We had fights.

MONTY: That sound like a man beat a woman to me.

RODDY: We had arguments, man, married people argument. I wouldn't expect you to understand anythin' like that.

MONTY: What?

RODDY: Man like you don't understand things like marriage an' commitment.

MONTY: I know about that, man, I was engaged one time, y'know.

RODDY: You? What you sayin'?

MONTY: Long time ago. Irish chick.

RODDY: Irish? You mean, the Irish woman you bring round for dinner one time?

MONTY: Dinner? Oh yes, same girl, man.

RODDY: The same girl you leave with us, go to the off licence to get wine and we don't hear from you for six months?

MONTY: (*Laughing.*) Same one. Tara O'Brien. Catholic girl come to London see black man for the first time.

TREVOR: An' that was you, right, uncle?

MONTY: She comes from one small village in the south. Bloody girl wouldn't give me nothin'. Gettin' engaged was the only way I could 'leggo beast'.

MONTY and TREVOR laugh.

RODDY: Poor woman.

MONTY: But tchoh! If there's one thing I know, I know that woman change when them marry, sir. In the end I had was to duss out still. She was too…too tough. She remind me of one of them chicken that take too long to cook.

RODDY: Broiler.

MONTY: Broiler? More like a Wrestler, man. The girl was big an' strong, coulda' kill me.

They all laugh.

MONTY dips into his pocket and pulls out his wallet. He pulls out a twenty pound note and offers it to RODDY.

RODDY: What's this?

MONTY: For the wine. I borrow the money from you, ennit.

RODDY: That was years ago, man.

MONTY: A debt is a debt still. Never let it be said Monty Griffiths never pay his debts.

RODDY: Thank you.

Pause.

MONTY: At least now you free you can fool-fool around with them toys whenever you want.

RODDY: How many times must I tell you they're not toys.

MONTY: Toys yes. They make them for kids.

RODDY: Them is not toys, man.

MONTY: Then what they is if not toys?

RODDY: Models.

TREVOR: C'mon, dad, they're the original toys. They got made in China written all over 'em.

MONTY: Alright!

RODDY: Read the box. It says model trains. An' for your information, they make them in Nottingham an' Birmingham.

TREVOR: Shanghai an' Hong Kong more-like.

RODDY: Old fashion British engineering, you can't beat it.

TREVOR: There's over a billion Chinese. They do it quicker, better an' cheaper. They eat anythin' that moves, an' they breed like hell.

They all laugh. RODDY holds up his latest engine.

RODDY: The R2275 Auther locomotive. Full workin' model. Eighty-seven to one ratio. British engineering at its best. You know it's four months I wait for them to deliver this engine?

RODDY sets the train running. They watch it for a while.

TREVOR: So what…?

MONTY: You gonna stop it?

RODDY: It's runnin' in.

MONTY: Runnin' in what?

RODDY: I just done tell you its a new engine. I have to run it in. I calculate it's twelve miles at thirty miles an hour. That's about half hour on this track.

TREVOR: Come on, dad, we can't shout over that racket for half hour.

MONTY: Turn it off, man! Feel like I'm in a kindergarten.

RODDY: (*Sighing.*) Aah well…Philistines.

RODDY reluctantly switches off the train.

MONTY: What a way the man love trains.

RODDY: Big trains in the daytime, little trains at nighttime, that's what Muriel used to say.

MONTY: The way you work that railways job, you become part of the fixtures and fittings. I thought you was never gonna leave.

RODDY: Them? Them swallow me up an' spit me out with a gold watch, 'Thank you very much, Mr Charles, thank you very much for giving us your whole life.' Little-little pension them give me not worth a raas.

They all laugh.

Aah, it's good to see you laugh like that.

TREVOR: Gettin' outa' that place is like Christmas or birthday, know what I mean?

RODDY: I really hope you'll stay out of trouble now, Trevor, I really do.

TREVOR: I hooked up with a couple of boys from in there. Gonna set up a studio, knock out a coupla' tunes. Even got a name for it already, check this: Her Majesty's Pleasure. How's that for a wicked album title?

RODDY: You wanna call it that?

TREVOR: Gonna do a bit of that garage with a hip hop flavour on a UK tip.

RODDY: Noise, sex, guns an' killing…

MONTY: That's what the young people like these days.

RODDY: You're a big man now, Trevor. You got two boys growin' up fast. Don't you think it's about time you sorted yourself out properly, like do somethin' sensible?

TREVOR: Like what?

RODDY: Settle down. Get a steady job.

TREVOR: Like what?

RODDY: You askin' me? Well, computers seem to be the in thing now, isn't it?

TREVOR: I done studied that already. Even went to a few of them computer classes on the inside. But can you see some white dude sayin', Right, Trevor, I want you to come in here an' take this thirty grand salary that I could be givin' to my nephew? No, aint gonna happen. Music's a street thing an' my thing is on street.

TREVOR performs an impromptu acapella music, a guttural rap hip hop rhythm.

RODDY: I can't stand it. It's not music.

TREVOR: It's ghetto culture, ennit. An' it's rakin' in the bread, you know why? Because guns, drugs, woman, money… That's it, right there. That's what everybody wants, even if they got it already.

There's a pause.

MONTY: Nat King Cole, The Ink Spots, The Platters, that's real music… (*Singing.*)
'When the twilight has gone
And the songbirds are singing
When the twilight has gone
You come into my heart
Cos here in my heart
Is where, you'll find
My Prayer…'
You hear that? Sweetboy music.

TREVOR: The twilight's definitely gone outa' that, Uncle, that's for sure.

They all laugh.

You know what I hate though?

RODDY: What's that?

TREVOR: Prison tea.

RODDY: Tea?

TREVOR: Yeah, man, prison tea. It taste like…prison. I never even used to like tea, but when you can't get it when you want it, you kinda' miss it, you get me. It's like pussy…

They laugh.

RODDY: You bring that prison tongue out here with you?

TREVOR: It grows on you, you get me.

RODDY: Well, now you can leave all that behind them high walls an' move on.

TREVOR: Yeah, you're right. (*Beat.*) You know what I really do fancy though? I really could do with a Chinese, man. Wan ton soup, noodles, sweet and sour…sweet and sour pussy, you get me.

They crack up again, more raucously.

MONTY: So wha' 'appen, you…?

TREVOR: What?

MONTY: You…you know, since you come out?

TREVOR: Don't be askin' me that, man.

MONTY: You don't get anythin', ennit?

TREVOR: Yeah!

MONTY: Don't believe you.

TREVOR: Want me to explain?

MONTY: No, sir. You don't have to explain anythin' to me.

TREVOR: Hear what, the first thing I did when I come out, right, I head up west. There's a little t'ing I know over there. She's like, not much of a looker but… You know when somethin' just sweet?

MONTY: Yeah man, know that.

TREVOR: She's got a sweet body, man. I had two years to make up. Rough night, dread…hey, I aint tellin' you my personal business.

MONTY: You don't have nothin' to tell.

MONTY and TREVOR laugh together raucously.

TREVOR: I was like a hungry man chowing down on that shit like it was cooked food.

MONTY: Yeah?

TREVOR: An' you know how the brothers love them food, dread.

A realisation dawns on RODDY.

RODDY: Trevor, when did you get out?

TREVOR: Eh?

MONTY: Black man must have to survive the system.

RODDY: When did they release you from that prison?

TREVOR: What?

RODDY: What? I thought we were goin' to at least try an' start on the right foot.

TREVOR: What you on about?

RODDY: That prison is at least a five hour drive from here. You went up west to see a girl, a little t'ing you call her…you wouldn't have had the time to do all that then arrive here just now.

MONTY and TREVOR shoot each other glances.

TREVOR: Alright, I got out yesterday. There was a party, a comin' home kind of thing. I couldn't not go.

RODDY: Why you lie to me? Why? You know, I don't need it. At this stage in my life I don't need worries. (*Beat.*) So what now Trevor? You gonna be a father to your children? Or you gonna continue this life, this in an' out, in an' out of jail business?

MONTY: This is not the right time, man.

RODDY: It is always the right time to do what is right.

MONTY: Let the man get used to bein' out before fillin' up his head with all this whatever whatever…

RODDY: Keep outa' this, man! This got nothin' to do with you. I already resign myself to the fact that my only son is a criminal.

MONTY: Criminal? He's a free man.

RODDY: Not everyone can walk the line like you. He get the chance to set things right, an' you latch onto him, lead him astray… So what, you can't find another lapdog jackass you can twist round your finger?

TREVOR becomes angry, stamping about the room.

TREVOR: Na na na, who you callin' jackass? Talkin' about me like I don't exist. I aint got nothin' to prove to nobody. Criminal? You come here an' wipe up white man's shit, don't expect me to do that…

RODDY: Don't talk to me like that in my house.

TREVOR: Cos hear what, I aint no fuckin' dibby dibby bwoy, you get me.

RODDY: You don't bastard hear me!

TREVOR: All a man like you good to let a next man an' man walk all over him…

RODDY: I said shut your mouth!

TREVOR: But it aint happenin' to me. Fuck with me, I'll just erase you like you was a fly botherin' me.

They square up to each other.

RODDY: You not in prison now. As big as you is, I'll put my fist in your mouth.

TREVOR: Yeah?

TREVOR pushes RODDY away.

Carry on with your fuckries! Your bullshit aint gonna fuck me up, seen.

RODDY: I warned you.

RODDY takes a step towards TREVOR with hand raised. But TREVOR pulls a knife from his back pocket keeping RODDY at arms length.

TREVOR: Stay away from me!

RODDY: What you gonna do with that, knife, Trevor? You gonna kill me?

TREVOR: Don't play the hero, dad. This is my rules now.

There's a searing standoff.

You're lucky I don't wet you…tellin' me what an' what I can and can't do.

After a moment MONTY intervenes.

MONTY: Alright Trevor, that's enough, put the knife away.

TREVOR lowers the knife. RODDY is stunned.

RODDY: It come to this? Huh? What's goin' on here? You the puppet master?

MONTY struts the floor.

MONTY: (*Alludes to the window.*) Look out there. Go on, look. You'll see a top of the range Benz park up on the street. This shirt is handmade. No machine, y'know. Stitched by hand. Shoes, Italian, handmade too. (*Beat.*) Look at this place. I wouldn't let my dog live here much less. An' look at you, you're a mess. What happened to you, man? In the old days we used to talk how we're gonna do this, gonna do that. This is the land of milk an' honey. All you get out of it is bread an' water.

RODDY: You come into my home and judge me? I worked for what little I have, for my family…

MONTY: Which family? You don't have family. You can't even breed. You're useless, man. What you have is trains. Big trains in the daytime. Little trains in the night-time. (*Beat.*) Huh! Trevor, come, let's go.

RODDY is stunned. MONTY is leaving. TREVOR hesitates.

TREVOR: You go, I just wanna…you know…

MONTY: I'll be in the car. Don't take too long here.

MONTY laughs facetiously as he exits.

TREVOR: (*Pause.*) Dad, I…

TREVOR goes to RODDY, but is shrugged aside.

RODDY: (*Sternly.*) You ever pull a knife, gun, whatever, on me again…you will have to use it, Trevor.

TREVOR: Sorry, I just lost it.

RODDY breathes a shallow sigh.

RODDY: You been to see your mother? Your kids? You just got out, an' you start again? (*Pause.*) I miss her, you know, your mother. After thirty-five years you find you do. She was barely seventeen when we met. Country girl, pretty little thing, used to get rushed. But I get there first. I did just start work for the Railways. We had a little one room place. Sometimes you wake up, you find six West Indian men sleepin' on the floor. Speedy, Johnny, Grantham, Mostel, Redman, an' Monty. The others find work, place to live, but Monty, no sir…workshy. Never liked work. Playboy…

TREVOR: This aint the sixties, dad. This is a new generation, when the black man a' go rise up an' dominate inna dis ya world, seen. (*Pause.*) There was this dread in there, always spoutin' that shit.

RODDY: For a minute there, I frighten.

TREVOR: (*Beat.*) It's lookin' like diamonds.

RODDY: What?

TREVOR: They're gettin' into diamonds.

RODDY: Who?

TREVOR: They want me to move them.

RODDY: They, who's they?

TREVOR: Does it matter? They is they, dad. They're big time an' they're offerin' me a loada' money. Diamonds are a girl's best friend, right?

RODDY is resigned to a state of helplessness. TREVOR stares at the model railway.

I used to hate them trains, you know, your trains. I used to hate 'em, didn't know why, but I hated 'em. It's cos they were yours. Anything you liked, I hated. (*Beat.*) Your trains. I used to get the scissors out, slip it under the cover and cut them wires. I was out of order. I used to watch you get them out and repair them. That used to piss me off even more. The fact that you never found out it was me breaking them…

RODDY: Well, actually…

RODDY stares at TREVOR, as if willing him on.

TREVOR: You knew?

RODDY: The more you cut, the more I repaired.

TREVOR: You knew an' you didn't do nothin'?

RODDY: I wanted to show you that no matter how tough you are, how bad you is, the institution is always tougher and badder. And it will always win. Always.

TREVOR: (*Pause.*) I just wanted you to talk to me, talk to me proper…you know, man to man, father to son. (*Beat.*) Uncle Monty used to come round, tellin' me about his runnings, used to make me laugh. I wanted you to do that. You were my dad. I wanted to laugh with my dad. But it always ended up with me gettin' a bollocking.

RODDY: Trevor…

RODDY moves across to TREVOR and throws his arms round him, kissing him on the cheek. They hug furiously.

TREVOR: Sorry, dad…

RODDY: No man…

TREVOR: It's true, you're the only one who really looks out for me an' I let you down.

RODDY: Water under the bridge, son. It's what you do from now that counts.

TREVOR: Yeah.

RODDY: (*Pause.*) Hey, I tell I get my new engine today? Four months I wait for it. I was just gonna run it in when you all arrive. You wanna see it run?

RODDY grabs hold of his train. TREVOR watches him set it down on the track.

TREVOR: (*Pause.*) Dad, I'm gonna bust a move.

RODDY: You goin'?

TREVOR: Gotta be back at the hostel by six… (*Shows the tag around his ankle.*) Curfew.

RODDY: You'll come see me, right?

TREVOR: You're my dad, aint ya?

RODDY and TREVOR shake hands.

RODDY: Good luck, son.

TREVOR: (*Beat.*) Dad, everything is everything.

TREVOR exits.

RODDY: Everything is everything.

RODDY goes over towards the kitchen area and peers out through the window.

Tiger, here Tiger. Stupid cat.

He finds his British Rail peaked cap and places it on his head. He picks up a red flag and a whistle. He blows his whistle and waves the flag.

The train now departing platform four is the late arriving nineteen forty-five Gatwick service…calling at Forest Hill, Norwood Junction, East Croydon, Haywards Heath and fast to Gatwick…

He switches on the train and watches the tiny train chug chug its way round the track.

Music: 'My Prayer' (The Righteous Brothers version).

Fade down lights.

The End.